SCENTED PLANTS

ANN BONAR

COLLINS

Products mentioned in this book

Benlate* + 'Activex'	contains	benomyl
'Bug Gun!'	contains	pyrethrum
'Keriroot'	contains	NAA + captan
'Nimrod'-T	contains	bupirimate/triforine
'Rapid'	contains	pirimicarb
'Roseclear'	contains	bupirimate/pirimicarb/triforine
'Weedol'	contains	diquat/paraquat

Products marked thus *'Sybol'* are trade marks of Imperial Chemical Industries plc
Benlate* is a registered trade mark of Du Pont's
Read the label before you buy: use pesticides safely.

Editors Maggie Daykin, Susanne Mitchell
Designer Chris Walker
Picture research Moira McIlroy

First published 1988 by
William Collins Sons & Co Ltd
London · Glasgow · Sydney
Auckland · Toronto · Johannesburg

British Library Cataloguing in Publication Data

Bonar, Ann
 Scented plants. —— (Collins Aura garden
 handbooks).
 1. Gardens, Fragrant
 I. Title
 635.9'68   SB454.3.F7

 ISBN 0–00–412395–6

Photoset by Bookworm Typesetting
Printed and bound in Hong Kong by Dai Nippon Printing
Company

Front cover: Sweet Peas by The Harry Smith Horticultural
Photographic Collection
Back cover: Garden Scene by Pat Brindley

CONTENTS

INTRODUCTION

Any garden is a delightful creation, whether small or large, and every garden is unique. Each is an intensely personal expression of its owner's concept of design, knowledge of plants and enthusiasm. One may overflow with exuberantly growing plants, another may be controlled and formal – this one be full of clipped evergreens and statuary, that one a riot of colours, and a third will be roses all the way.

LEFT Plants whose flowers are fragrant at night, such as tobacco plants (seen in the foreground) are attractive to moths, which fly at night.

BELOW Many pink-flowered plants, such as the hardy miniature cyclamen, are scented.

As anyone even remotely connected with gardening knows, the possibilities are endless, and among the most delightful of these is to indulge oneself in growing plants with scented flowers or leaves. A garden without fragrance has no soul – it is a quality which adds immeasurably to the delights of a garden, and what is more, the garden centres don't seem to have caught on to the idea of charging a little extra for a plant that bears fragrant flowers.

Pollination factor It is nearly always the flower that is the scented part of a plant. This is to do with pollination; insects are the main pollinators, and one of their attractants is aroma or perfume. Plants which are self-fertile are rarely scented; for instance, the poppy family sets seeds extremely freely, so do mulleins (verbascum), but practically none of them carry perfume. Scented flowers are almost always pollinated by butterflies and moths. Bees are attracted by the appearance of a flower and particularly by the colour blue; birds are attracted by bright colours such as red and yellow.

Subtle colours Scented flowers are seldom strongly coloured. In fact many of them are white or yellow, such as mahonia, orange blossom and the yellow azalea. If you come across a selection of colours for a particular genus – such as the freesias – the white and yellow varieties are likely to be the most strongly scented. Pink is another colour which often crops up in combination with a scented flower – garden pinks and carnations, roses, cyclamen and peonies, all encompass a range from palest pastel to crushed strawberry, and have perfume in some degree. Pinkish-purple, lilac, purple and mauve make another range of colours associated with flowers carrying perfume; lavender, sweet rocket and violets being among the most intensely scented. Interestingly, many of these flowers are now regarded as the old cottage garden plants.

Winged visitors Flowers which give out perfume during the day are visited mainly by butterflies, but the many plants whose flowers are frag-

rant at night, such as night-scented stock and tobacco plants, are attractive to the moths, which fly at night.

Plants also have aromas and fragrances in their leaves and, occasionally, their roots. The flowers of *Iris florentina* smell of chocolate, and the roots are powerfully perfumed with violet when dried – they provide orris root.

Many plants, notably herbs such as tarragon, lovage and rock roses have pungently aromatic leaves. Some have leaves with flower fragrances – there are two pelargoniums with rose-scented foliage – and some smell very much like fruits. Lemon balm is one, and bergamot (*Monarda didyma*) named for the bergamot orange, is another.

ABOVE *Buddleia davidii*, the butterfly bush is so-called because it attracts butterflies, such as the Red Admiral.

LEFT Many herbs, which can be most attractively grown in their own special garden, have pungently aromatic leaves.

USING SCENTED PLANTS

Mainly herbaceous perennials are used for planting beds, borders and islands. These are plants which live from year to year but whose flowers die down in autumn, in most cases together with the leaves. Some are evergreen, however, and continue to provide interest in the garden through the otherwise bare months of winter. Scented perennials include daylily species (hemerocallis), one of the plantain lilies, *Hosta plantaginea,* evening primroses (oenothera), peonies, and bergamot (*Monarda didyma*).

Several roses, such as *Rosa gallica* and its varieties, make excellent hedges. The flowers of *R.gallica* have a typical old-rose perfume and it makes a superb informal hedge. It is also amenable to being cut back if necessary.

Surprisingly, there are not a lot of herbaceous perennials that are scented, but there are other plants with this quality which can be used in borders and island beds. For instance, violets – evergreen as well – pinks and carnations whose silvery grey foliage looks lovely all year, and lily of the valley, all perennial but in a slightly different category. Bulbs can be heavily fragrant; the Regal lily is one example, and hyacinths are another.

Scented plants grown from seed and for only one flowering season are useful for filling odd spaces while perennials grow to their full size. The fragrance of sweet peas is difficult to beat, and you can grow them like small bushes, 60 or 90cm (2 or 3ft) high, as well as the classic 1.8m (6ft) cordon types. Seed-sown stocks and tobacco plants are often used for bedding designs as well as in the role of space-fillers.

Use these scented plants, of whatever type, mixed with the others, so that fragrance comes from some part of the bed or border all summer. You can also use scented shrubs, which will give the beds height as well as fragrance, and even more interest by virtue of their different shapes, their leaves and their autumn colouring.

Shrubberies, hedges and specimen trees Shrubberies can be delightfully enclosed and secluded areas of the garden, sheltered from wind and collecting the sun so that many otherwise tender plants can be grown close by. A great number of shrubs have long-lasting scented flowers; some are deciduous, some evergreen, and of such variety that there are bound to be half a dozen to suit any garden.

Witch-hazel and *Viburnum fragrans* perfume the midwinter air, the yellow azalea haunts the nostrils in late spring, and early summer is heady with the fragrance of syringa. Trees such as laburnum and magnolia add height to the canopy of garden plants, taking their rightful place as handsome specimens on lawns or against walls.

For mixed borders there are plenty of small shrubs. A small version of syringa or mock orange, *Philadelphus* 'Manteau d'Hermine', flowering in early summer, grows to only 90cm (3ft); and *Skimmia japonica* 'Fragrans', the same height, blooms from early to mid spring. Rock roses produce their fleeting, saucer-shaped flowers through late spring and early summer on plants only 60cm (2ft) in the cultivar *Cistus* 'Decumbens'.

Hedges are an integral part of any garden, whether used as boundaries or internal dividers. They are composed of trees which remain compact and tidy with clipping, or of shrubs, either formally trained or allowed to grow more or less naturally. The musk roses make a glorious hedge, overflowing with fragrance and colour in midsummer, while gorse provides an excellent defence against the outside world, its bright golden, vanilla-scented flowers appearing in late winter, and most welcome.

LEFT Lavender is aromatic in all its parts and is often used as a low hedge.

ABOVE The evergreen shrub, *Osmanthus delavayi*, has fragrant blooms.

LEFT Climbing and rambling roses can be trained up pillars of various kinds as well as pergolas.

ABOVE Several varieties of climbing rose will provide scent on the house walls.

Roses The old shrub roses have heavenly perfumes unrivalled by any other rose; indeed two of them – a damask rose and a gallica variety – are the commercial sources of Attar of Roses. Most have a graceful and informal habit of growth which needs little pruning beyond removal of any dead or diseased shoots, and grow to between 75cm and 1.8m (2½ and 6ft) tall. Some groups, such as the Bourbons, have repeat flowering through the summer and so do some of the modern hybrids of this type, e.g. 'Graham Thomas'.

They blend well with mixed borders or in shrubberies with grass paths, and as specimens in lawns. They alleviate the formality of paving if they are planted in spaces within it, or in long borders, perhaps at the sides of a terrace.

Large-flowered (hybrid tea) and cluster-flowered (floribunda) roses flower more heavily and for much longer, but have stiff, upright growth. If you like formality, they can complement paving, but grown in beds and borders, especially when they are without foliage or flowers, they need 'softening'. Small spreading plants growing close to them will help, especially when planted in beds to themselves. Primroses, border auriculas, border pinks and carnations, and violets are a few examples, and most of these plants have evergreen leaves.

Rose gardens could be an intriguing mixture of modern hybrids, the old shrub roses and climbing roses, the whole enclosed by hedges of musk roses. Climbers and ramblers can be trained up wooden or brick pillars to make focal points over arches, and along pergolas. Pillars can be linked by ropes or chains along which the long shoots of ramblers can be trained.

Cottage garden plants So many of the flowering plants which have been grown for centuries – the valued antiques of the garden – had and still have a powerful fragrance, and were grown as much for that as for their attractive appearance and ease of cultivation. The cottage pinks, called clove gilly flowers in an Elizabethan herbal, are typical of this group, and are ideal, since they provide pretty, fragrant flowers in summer, evergrey foliage, and are not difficult to increase.

The great, blowsy peonies of *Paeonia lactiflora* can also trace their cultivation back to the reign of the first Queen Elizabeth, as does the Madonna lily, *Lilium candidum,* flowering after the peony in early to midsummer. Wallflowers have been grown from time immemorial, and so has the daphne called mezereon, a very early shrub that flowers in late winter.

Lilies of the valley, sweet rocket, daylilies and heliotrope would all have been grown in a delightful jumble, along with honeysuckle, evening primroses and night-scented stocks. Most of these are the original unhybridized species. Our own modern flowers are bred to be big and brightly coloured, as though garden plants have no other charms, such as a delightful fragrance, attractive leaves, interesting habits of growth and so on.

The essence of cottage gardening is that it does not have an underlying design. The most that you can say about its style is that it is informal, with a high degree of inconsequentiality. Plants are stuffed in wherever there is a space, as they had to be in the old days when gardens were tiny. But this casual treatment should not get out of hand so they become an untidy tangle. Certainly, plants can grow through other plants, but none should be allowed to overpower another.

LEFT The aromatic thymes are 'at home' in situations such as rose and cottage gardens.

ABOVE Primroses, with their fresh, delicate fragrance, are often found in cottage gardens.

Herb gardens There is nothing more delightful than a fragrant herb garden with the sun blazing down on it in summer. The pungent mixture of scents announces the garden's presence long before it is seen, and the blend of perfumes and aromatic oils in the air attract an enormous variety of pollinating insects such as moths and butterflies.

Herb gardens can be a collection of beds or a single border; they can be made by grouping together containers or by planting herbs in spaces left between paving on a patio or terrace. Such a garden can look highly decorative and brings the various fragrances nearer to the house.

Many herbs have unusual foliage and with carefully chosen, neighbourly planting, contrasts in leaf form can be highlighted. Fennel has delicate feathery foliage, bronze-coloured in one of its varieties; absinth (*Artemisia absinthium*) has silvery-grey leaves, and lemon balm is beautifully golden-variegated in its varietal form.

Flowers, also, are part of the herb scene; they include lavender, rosemary, the scented-leaved pelargoniums, and orris root (*Iris florentina*). The curry plant has silver leaves and bright yellow flowers, and thymes almost flower themselves to death.

To keep all this abundance under control, formal paved or gravel paths are a help in defining the beds, whether they are set in a chessboard pattern or like the spokes of a wheel or in the form of a maze. Miniature formal hedges of southernwood, kept clipped, can surround beds laid out in knot designs, or thymes alternating with pinks can be used to confine taller and/or more rampant growers.

LEFT AND ABOVE Herb gardens can be highly attractive as well as aromatic, as many herbs have colourful or attractive foliage and flowers. Good contrasts can be achieved.

One excellent evergreen carpeting plant for a scented lawn is the creeping thyme, *Thymus serpyllum*. The flowers come in a variety of shades during summer.

Scented lawns What could be nicer than to walk on a carpet which gives off aromatic scents with each footfall? Outdoor carpeting plants can be the source of such a desirable quality and, even if they cannot take quite the same wear as the average lawn, can be used for paths in herb gardens, to cover the floor of an arbour or to clothe small sitting-out areas. The plants suitable for the purpose may not survive regular trafficking across them and certainly not the play of children and pets, but otherwise they make an adequate and delightful covering all year.

One excellent evergreen covering plant is creeping thyme, *Thymus serpyllum*. Its tiny, dark green leaves grow in pairs on long running stems lying flat on the soil and rooting as they grow, and in summer the tiny pink and purple flowers will transform the green carpet into a brilliant patchwork of variations of these colours. Plant it in mid spring on well-drained soil in a sunny place, spacing the plants 15cm (6in) apart, and keep it weed-free while it is becoming established.

A second aromatic plant for scented lawns is chamomile, *Chamaemelum nobile*. The standard version has white daisy flowers, but there is a non-flowering form called 'Treneague' which can be kept low-growing and mat forming with monthly clipping – not mowing. The frond-like foliage remains green in dry weather, even on light soil, though such soil should have peat mixed into it before planting. Plants are spaced at 7.5–10cm (3–4in) apart, in spring, and hand-weeding will be necessary until a complete cover forms.

Other plants for aromatic lawns are *Mentha requienii*, with tiny round, peppermint-scented leaves, and pennyroyal in its creeping form, *Mentha pulegium decumbens,* pungent and 'minty'. Both prefer average to moist soils and are happiest in sun or a little light shade.

SOILS AND PLANTING

Whatever plant you are dealing with, the choice and preparation of the soil before planting are crucial. Always try to suit the plant to the soil; attempting to grow it in a type which is alien will result in problems all the plant's life. If in doubt, plant in a dryish soil rather than one that is always inclined to be wet. You can always water, if need be.

Plants should be suited to soil type so, before planting, test the soil with the aid of a simple soil-testing kit, to determine acidity or alkalinity. Some plants need an acid or lime-free soil.

Soil-testing Another aspect to take into account is whether the soil is chalky, that is, whether it has an alkaline reaction when tested. Some plants will not grow in such soils; they need acid conditions. Azaleas magnolias and some of the lilies are examples.

Soil can quite well be alkaline even if it does not contain chalk, and you can test its reaction easily with a simple soil-testing kit obtainable at any garden centre or shop.

Adapting the soil If you want to reduce the acidity of a soil, the instructions with the soil-testing kit will tell you how much lime to use, but reducing the alkalinity of soil is much more difficult and takes several years to achieve.

In order to grow well, plants also need a soil which has a good structure, and is neither sticky and like plasticine when wet, nor gritty and stony. These two extremes indicate too much clay or too much sand, and most soils contain some of each, together with other ingredients such as peat, chalk, silt and organic matter. The last-mentioned is extremely important; it is this, in the form of rotting animal and vegetative remains – mostly the latter – which ensures that a good structure is maintained.

Organic matter rots down to provide humus, a dark crumbly substance that absorbs moisture and helps to collect the soil particles into crumbs. This in turn creates spaces in the soil, thus allowing air to be present and excess water to drain through into the subsoil quickly.

14

Before putting in almost any kind of plant, it pays to dig over the planting area in advance and to mix in rotted organic matter, such as garden compost, farm manure if obtainable, poultry deep litter, spent mushroom compost, 'Forest Bark' Ground and Composted or peat, though this contains only a minute quantity of plant nutrients. General compound fertilizers in granular or powder form can also be added if necessary, depending on the type of plant and soil.

Planting shrubs The best time to plant bare-rooted, deciduous shrubs and trees is in autumn or spring. Evergreens grow better if planted in spring. However, container-grown plants can be put in at any time, provided summer plantings are kept well watered until established.

Prepare the site a month in advance by digging one or two spades deep and mixing in organic matter or some 'Forest Bark' Ground and Composted. If it is an old town soil or a very well-drained one, fork in a fertilizer such as Growmore a week in advance, or use a soil conditioner based on seaweed.

If necessary, put a supporting stake in the planting hole first, and put in the plant to a level that leaves the soil mark on the main stem on a level with the soil surface, and spread the roots out round the plant to their full extent. Crumble soil in over the roots, then fill in the hole and tread the soil down. Finally, rake the surface and water in.

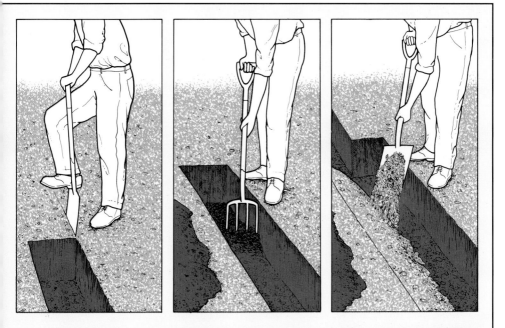

Prepare the ground well before planting. Start by digging a 30cm (1ft) wide trench to a spade's depth. Leave the soil removed on the far side.

Loosen the soil in the bottom of the trench. Add manure or garden compost and 'Forest Bark' Composted, and a compound fertilizer if necessary.

Take out a second trench. Throw the soil forward into the first (turn the soil as you do this). Continue to end, there using the soil from first trench to fill in.

Herbaceous perennials are mostly planted direct from containers, although sometimes they are bare root (as shown here), especially your own divisions. First space out the plants, at the correct distance apart, in a group. Then make the hole deep and wide enough to take the roots. Spread out the roots well and work fine soil between and around them. Finally, firm in the plant really well.

Planting herbaceous perennials
These are mostly planted direct from containers. If the garden is a cold one or the soil is heavy and moisture-retaining, plant in spring; otherwise plant in early to mid autumn. Dig to about one spade deep, preparing the site in advance as with shrubs, then follow the same general principles, being very careful not to bruise or injure fleshy roots when actually planting.

The soil need not be dug so deep for small perennials, 15cm (6in) is often sufficient, unless they are of the rock-garden type or have grey or silver leaves. Such plants particularly like good drainage, and deeper digging with the addition of grit will help to ensure that they enjoy a long and healthy life.

Planting bulbs Spring-flowering bulbs are planted in early to late autumn, the earlier the better; autumn-flowering ones in midsummer, and summer-flowering kinds in spring. Most bulbs have developed this specialized form to see them through very dry weather conditions and/or rocky soil, and a sprinkling of coarse sand at the bottom of the hole when planting will enable them to establish without problems from basal rotting. Organic matter is not necessary. A good rule of thumb for planting is to plant the bulb at a depth twice the length of the bulb.

Growing from seed Hardy annual seeds can be sown in autumn or spring. The advantage of autumn sowing is that they flower much earlier, but unfortunately not many are hardy enough to overwinter. The soil for the seeds must be fine, the texture of small breadcrumbs, and needs careful preparation: digging, breaking up the lumps with a fork, treading, and raking to make the soil even finer, and level.

Seeds germinate best in light soil. If it is heavy, you can cheat by replacing some of the topsoil with potting compost; it saves time and gives the seedlings a good start. Sow the seed thinly and evenly on to moist soil or compost, then cover lightly and firm down. Water with a fine rose if no rain occurs within two days of sowing.

After germination, when the seedlings have become large enough to handle, thin out to 2.5cm (1in) apart, and a second time when the leaves are touching.

Biennials, sown in late spring, can be thinned once to about 10cm (4in), and then transplanted to their flowering places in mid autumn. Half-hardy seeds to provide bedding plants flowering midsummer to early autumn should be sown in a propagator with a temperature of about 16–18°C (61–64°F) in late winter to early spring, using moist seed compost in pots, pans or seed trays. Sow thinly and cover with black plastic sheet, then when the first true leaf can be seen, prick out into seed-trays 5cm (2in) apart in potting compost. Plant out after hardening off, in early summer.

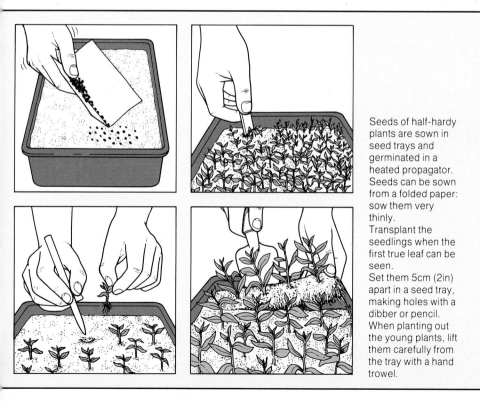

Seeds of half-hardy plants are sown in seed trays and germinated in a heated propagator. Seeds can be sown from a folded paper: sow them very thinly.
Transplant the seedlings when the first true leaf can be seen.
Set them 5cm (2in) apart in a seed tray, making holes with a dibber or pencil.
When planting out the young plants, lift them carefully from the tray with a hand trowel.

In any garden, there are two jobs that always need to be done at regular intervals, and the scented garden is no exception. One of these tasks is weeding, the other is deadheading.

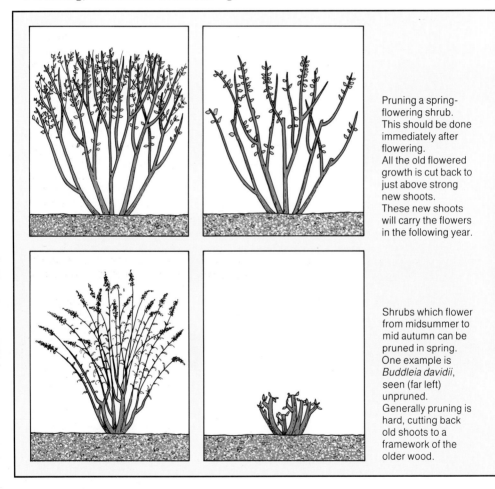

Pruning a spring-flowering shrub. This should be done immediately after flowering.
All the old flowered growth is cut back to just above strong new shoots.
These new shoots will carry the flowers in the following year.

Shrubs which flower from midsummer to mid autumn can be pruned in spring. One example is *Buddleia davidii*, seen (far left) unpruned.
Generally pruning is hard, cutting back old shoots to a framework of the older wood.

Weeding Weeds grow from seeds blown in by the wind, carried by birds or animals, walked in on one's own feet, or carried in on tools and soils of container-grown plants. Hand weeding is easy' for seedlings and small weeds without disturbing the seedlings of cultivated plants, but difficult weeds need spraying. For epidemics of small weeds you can use 'Weedol'. For spot-weeding and persistent weeds, spot treating with glyphosate is the best answer; but avoid contact with cultivated plants.

Deadheading is the removal of faded flowers. Nothing detracts from the appearance of a plant more than clusters of brown-petalled, drooping flowers. Besides, removal encourages the production of more flowers. Take off the spent flowers down to the first or second leaf on the stem (going round the garden about once a week) and put them on the compost heap. The only time when this routine deadheading should not be carried out is when you want a particular plant to produce seeds.

Pruning only applies to shrubs and climbers on the whole, though trees occasionally need some cutting back. Herbaceous plants need not so much pruning, as cutting back also.

SHRUBS that flower any time from spring to the end of early summer are better for pruning off the flowered growth back to just above strong new shoots, which will carry the flowers next year. Those that flower from midsummer to mid autumn need not be pruned until spring, in the same way. They will flower on shoots produced in the same spring. The winter-flowering shrubs generally grow slowly and need not be pruned, but remove dead and damaged stems, and weak ones, and otherwise thin out as appropriate to avoid crowding.

CLIMBERS can be left more or less to themselves, beyond cutting back sufficiently to tidy them up and keep them within their alloted space. The same applies to trees – a single branch may become too vigorous and need removal.

HERBACEOUS PERENNIALS finish their growing season with a tangle of dead and dying flower stems. These can either be removed to ground level and put on the compost heap, or left for the winter as protection, and

removed in the spring as the new growth appears.

If mulching is done in mid spring, it prevents weeds from growing, and keeps the soil moist, provided it was already in that condition.

Plant health Many scented and aromatic plants are not attacked by pests and diseases, and if plants are infected, it is a sign that their growing conditions are not suitable. Just moving them to a different part of the garden could make all the difference; alternatively much can be done with finger and thumb control of small pests – simply wipe them off. Otherwise, if the problem is widespread, use a pesticide, but be sure to follow the instructions on the label with regard to its application. Also follow these general safety guidelines:
- Avoid spraying open blooms.
- Best times to spray are early morning and late evening when few insects are around.
- Do not spray when it is windy.
- Do not spray in direct sunlight.
- Store chemical concentrates in a safe, dry place, out of the reach of children and pets.
- Read the label carefully. Always use the dilution rate and method of application recommended.

To control aphids (greenfly and blackfly) and other sap-sucking insects use a 'Bug Gun!', which contains pyrethrum. 'Rapid' (containing pirimicarb) will control aphids and not affect bees and ladybirds.

Recommended fungicides for dealing with most common fungal diseases in the garden are Benlate + 'Activex' (contains benomyl) or 'Nimrod'-T and 'Roseclear' (containing bupirimate and triforine). The last product also contains pirimicarb for aphid control on roses without harm to beneficial insects.

PROPAGATION

Many plants do their own increasing; for instance, narcissi produce offsets (small bulbs) at the base of the parent; violets put out plantlets on the end of runners, and mint has creeping stems which root, and then produce leaves. But even if plants are not so obliging, the standard propagation techniques are quite easy to learn.

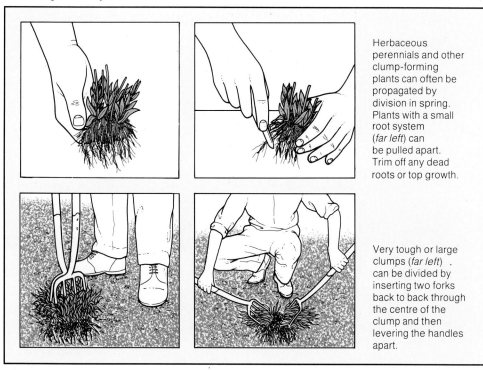

Herbaceous perennials and other clump-forming plants can often be propagated by division in spring. Plants with a small root system (*far left*) can be pulled apart. Trim off any dead roots or top growth.

Very tough or large clumps (*far left*) . can be divided by inserting two forks back to back through the centre of the clump and then levering the handles apart.

Division Where plants become large they can often be divided without harming them, particularly if they are herbaceous perennials. Dig them up, cut down through the middle of the crown with a sharp knife, then discard the centre, which is the oldest and therefore the least vigorous and floriferous part, planting out the newly-divided plants. This is best done in spring.

Layering Shrubs grow from suckers from the base, but more often will layer themselves naturally, that is, a stem, a low-growing part of which is lying on the soil, will root into it, at which stage it can be cut off and transplanted as a separate plant. Otherwise, you can initiate layering in summer or early autumn. First make a slanting cut partially through the underside of a pliable stem, opposite a joint, then pull it down to the ground, and peg it down before covering the area of the cut with a layer of soil. Leave until strong roots have formed before separating the new plant from its parent and siting it elsewhere.

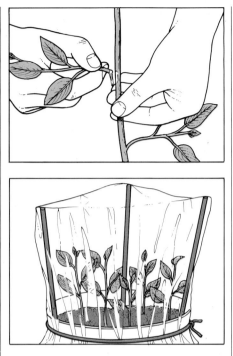

TOP Taking a semi-ripe heel cutting of a shrub by removing it with some of the older wood.

ABOVE The cuttings can be rooted in pots enclosed in a clear polythene bag supported on sticks.

Stem cuttings Shrubs can also be increased by stem cuttings, of which there are three main types.

• Soft or tip cuttings consist of the end of a new shoot which is still growing and is soft and green. The top 7.5–10cm (3–4in) are cut off and the cut end trimmed cleanly just below a leaf or a pair of leaves by removing the lowest leaves. The cutting is then inserted to half its length in a pot or other container of moist cuttings compost such as 'Kericompost', and the atmosphere around it kept humid by placing a plastic bag or tent of clear polythene sheet over the pot, held clear of the plant by three or four small sticks or canes round the perimeter. 'Keri-root' rooting powder (contains NAA and captan) can be used for more certain root production, and the cutting kept at 18°C (64°F) or more until rooting occurs in 1-4 weeks.

• Semi-hardwood or semi-ripe cuttings are taken later in the summer, in mid to late summer, between 7.5–15cm (3–6in) long; again, take them from the ends of new shoots, but choose those which have begun to turn brown and firm at the base. Sometimes these are not cut back but torn off with a sliver of bark from the parent stem still intact; these are called 'heel cuttings' and the extra tissue is an additional insurance for successful rooting. The 'heel' is trimmed and the two lower pairs of leaves removed as described for softwood cuttings and the prepared cutting is then potted in the same way. Both these and soft cuttings are potted on after rooting and overwintered under cover before being planted outdoors the following spring. Rooting can be speeded up by the use of a hormone rooting powder such as 'Keriroot'.

• Hardwood or ripe cuttings are made in autumn, when new shoots are brown and firm almost to the tip. They should be about 25cm (10in) long after the soft tip has been removed, and are rooted outdoors in a sheltered place, where they are left for a year and then planted where they are to grow.

Seeds All cuttings produce plants exactly like the parent, but if you collect seeds from your plants and sow them, they will germinate either like one or other parent, or be quite different, possibly improved. Such seed should be collected when ripe, that is, when the seedpods are opening, the seed is brown or black and falls easily. Then remove its protective coating and sow at once, as viability may not last very long.

SIXTY SCENTED PLANTS

The selection that follows is a happy blend of both aromatic and fragrant plants. Annuals, bulbs, perennials and shrubs are described here in all their variety, giving you a range of plants suitable for any situation in the garden – whether it is clothing the house walls, furnishing an arbour or pergola, planting up a herb garden or arranging a bed of sweet-smelling flowers under a window. This is purely a personal choice but its very versatility will, I hope, please many people.

Artemisia

Several artemisias are grown for their aromatic leaves, which are mostly valued for culinary uses. *A. dracunculus* is tarragon, with a peculiarly spicy flavour all its own. *A. abrotanum* is lad's love or southernwood, with pungently aromatic, feathery leaves, now grown as an ornamental plant but once used as a vermifuge – 'Lambrook Silver' has silvery-grey leaves. *A. absinthium* or wormwood has bitterly aromatic, grey-green foliage, which provides the absinth used in making liqueurs and aperitifs.

Tarragon grows to approximately 60 × 60cm (2 × 2ft), lad's love to 90 × 60cm (3 × 2ft), and wormwood to 90 × 38cm (36 × 15in). All need well-drained soil and sun; tarragon also requires protection in winter. Increase by seed, division, or by heeled cuttings (lad's love).

Buddleia davidii

Also called the butterfly bush, the common name suggests at once that it is scented; in mid- to late summer it will attract a mass of butterflies when the long, purple flower spikes are in full bloom.

An easily grown hardy shrub, 2.4 × 1.8m (8 × 6ft), it will grow in most soils and sun or a little shade. Prune hard in early spring, cutting the previous year's new shoots back to leave a few centimetres (inches) of stem. Pretty varieties are: 'Empire Blue', 'Black Knight', deep purple and strongly perfumed, 'Harlequin' with yellow-variegated leaves and purple flowers, and 'White Cloud'. Increase by hardwood cuttings.

Buddleia davidii, butterfly bush.

Artemisia 'Lambrook Silver' has attractive aromatic foliage.

Calycanthus floridus

The allspice is a large, spreading shrub or small tree, also called Californian allspice. It has untidy, dull red and purple flowers rather like miniature old-fashioned mopheads, with an extremely strong and fruity scent, most unusual for a flower. The leaves and wood, by contrast, are redolent of camphor. Flowering continues through late June, July and August; height and spread are about 2.4m (8ft), more in good positions of sun and shelter from cold wind. Well-drained soil containing peat is important. Increase by layering.

Chamaemelum nobile

Chamomile is a strongly aromatic herb in all its parts, and can be used for a small lawn, provided it does not have to bear too much traffic. The bruising caused by treading releases the plant's aromatic oils, producing a delightfully pungent fragrance.

The species has white daisy flowers on 23cm (9in) stems in summer, but for lawns a non-flowering strain called 'Treneague', clips well and spreads sideways to form mats about 30cm (1ft) wide. Plant 30cm (1ft) apart if grown as specimen plants and provide a sandy soil and open position. Increase from seed or rooted cuttings ('Treneague' only by the latter method).

Cheiranthus cheiri

Wallflowers have the sweetest and most evocative of perfumes, especially strong in the hot sun. Lasting in flower for five or six weeks, colours are generally yellows, orange-reds and shades of velvety brown, but there are also mixtures in the purple, pink and wine range.

Wallflowers are biennials, grow to 25–45cm (10–18in) tall, spread to 20–30cm (8–12in), and are excellent for filling in spaces until permanent border plants grow to take their place. Sow seed in late spring in a nursery bed, and thin to 10cm (4in) apart; pinch out the tips of the shoots when about 15cm (6in) tall. Transplant to permanent positions in the early autumn, spacing them approximately 20cm (8in) apart.

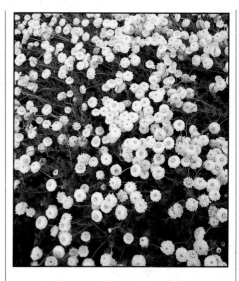

Double-flowered Chamaemelum.

Cheiranthus or wallflower.

Chimonanthus praecox

Winter sweet is a slow-growing shrub reaching about 2.7 × 2.1m (9 × 7ft) in ten years. It flowers in early-mid winter on bare branches, the pale yellow, narrow-petalled flowers having a purple centre and being heavily scented.

Give it a sunny place, preferably close to a wall sheltered from north and east wind. The soil must be well-drained, and for the best results should be fertile and sandy. If wall-grown, prune in late February to remove weak and crowded shoots, and cut back lightly some of the strongest growing ones. Increase by layering or seed.

Choisya ternata

Another shrub, this one is called the Mexican orange blossom because its large clusters of white flowers in the late spring and early summer are heavily and sweetly fragrant in the same way. It is one of the shapeliest shrubs, forming naturally into a nicely rounded evergreen bush about 1.8 × 1.8m (6 × 6ft) in size, with glossy evergreen leaflets in threes. A new variety, called 'Sundance', has pale yellow leaves and is slower growing.

Choisya needs the protection of a sunny wall, and is damaged or killed in severe winters. It needs good soil drainage. Pruning is not required except to keep it in bounds; do this in early spring if necessary. Increase by semi-hardwood cuttings.

Cistus

The evergreen rock roses are natives of the Mediterranean region, and flower profusely for several weeks – each flower lasts only a day but there are so many that the bush is constantly covered in them. Pink, white, magenta and rose are the main colours of the saucer-shaped

Choisya ternata, heavily scented.

The aromatic *Cistus laurifolius*.

flowers; the foliage is evergreen, sometimes slightly sticky.

Cistus × lusitanicus 'Decumbens', 90cm (3ft), has large white flowers with a crimson blotch at the base of the petals, *C. × purpureus,* 90–120cm (3–4ft) is rose-purple flowered, and *C. laurifolius* has white flowers on bushes 1.8–2.4m (6–8ft) high. These three have aromatic foliage, the smell of which is particularly marked on hot, sunny days. All are fairly hardy, need well-drained soil, and sunny, sheltered places. Increase by cuttings in summer; pruning is not required.

Citrus

The evergreen-leaved orange and lemon family is not only renowned for its fruits, but for its white flowers in mid spring – they perfume the air for many yards round and a citrus orchard in full flower can be smelt long before it is seen.

Citrus trees can be grown in tubs kept under protection in winter and early spring, then put in the garden in a sunny, sheltered place for the summer and early autumn. Give them a soil-based potting compost such as John Innes No 3; provide drainage holes and use containers at least 30cm (1ft) diameter. Water well in summer, particularly in dry spells. No pruning is required.

Convallaria majalis, for shade.

Convallaria majalis

If you have a shady corner, lily of the valley will thrive in it. Its uniquely sweetly scented, small, white bell flowers will lighten the shade in late spring, and its sheath-like leaves cover the soil until autumn. Easily grown, convallaria spreads underground by creeping stems and does best in moist soil. Increase by digging up individual crowns in autumn and replanting. There is a lovely variety called *rosea* whose little flowers are faintly flushed with pink.

Cyclamen

The large-flowered pot plant cyclamen have no fragrance, but there are eleven species with scented flowers. Among these are *C. creticum,* spring-flowering, *C. persicum* (also spring-flowering) the parent of the large-flowered kinds, *C. hederifolium* (syn. *C. neapolitanum*), autumn-flowering, and *C. purpurascens,* summer-flowering.

All require good drainage, a little shade in summer, and shelter from wind. Protection from winter cold ensures that the foliage remains evergreen. Once planted, they are best left alone, and will increase slowly of their own accord, forming a large patch of naturalized tubers that have grown from seed.

Cyclamen hederifolium.

Cytisus battandieri

This member of the broom family will grow vigorously against a south-facing wall to about 3 × 3m (10 × 10ft), or in the open garden, provided it is sheltered from wind.

It needs sun, and will produce silky pinnate leaves and, in June, fat, yellow spikes like lamb's tails of heavily fragrant flowers, smelling of pineapple. Good soil drainage is important, but pruning need only be done to keep it in bounds and well shaped, in early spring. Increase from semi-hardwood cuttings.

Daphne

Daphnes are shrubs, all with heavily scented flowers. The mezereon, *D. mezereum*, is a British native which flowers mid winter to early spring and is deciduous, slowly growing to 90 × 60cm (3 × 2ft). It has purplish red flowers, followed by poisonous, red berries. *D. cneorum* has fragrant, pink flowers in mid to late spring, on stems about 30cm (1ft) tall; spread is 90cm (3ft).

Daphnes do not like transplanting, so always buy container-grown ones; they respond badly to pruning and should be left alone. Good drainage is essential, but moisture is also important, and some peat mixed with the soil when planting is helpful. A sunny or slightly shaded spot are equally suitable.

Dianthus

Border carnations and pinks are among the loveliest of garden flowers, and among the most strongly scented, too. Shades of pink, red, salmon, yellow, white, magenta, crimson and apricot are their colours, set off by silvery grey foliage which has the additional merit of being evergrey. Height is 23–90cm (9–36in) and spread can be up to 45cm (1½ft). Generally, carnations are larger plants than pinks, which are shorter, have more delicate foliage and smaller flowers.

'Mrs Sinkins' is a heavily scented, old-fashioned, white-flowered pink; 'Doris' is a modern hybrid, salmon-pink and easily grown. Border carnations are many and varied, but 'Perfect Clove', deep crimson, and 'Candy Clove', white and rose, are both very fragrant. Soil must be well-drained, fertile, and preferably alkaline, and a sunny position gives the best results. Increase by layering, in late summer, cuttings in midsummer or seed in mid spring.

Spring-blooming *Daphne cneorum*.

Old-fashioned pink (dianthus).

Foeniculum vulgare has attractive flowers and aromatic leaves.

Erysimum

The alpine wallflower (also known as the Siberian wallflower) *E.* × *allionii (Cheiranthus × allionii),* has bright orange flowers lasting for many weeks in spring and summer, on stems up to 60cm (2ft) tall, but more commonly seen at 30cm (1ft), with a spread of about 15cm (6in). A variant is 'Golden Gem', which though perennial, flowers so profusely as to kill it. It is best grown, like its relative, as a biennial, and cultivated in the same way.

Foeniculum vulgare

The fennels are highly aromatic culinary herbs, to 150 × 50cm (5ft × 20in), with finely divided, feathery leaves. Flat yellow heads of flowers appear midsummer and the plant is perennial. There is a variety with bronze foliage – a handsome plant in a mixed border. The aniseed aroma of the leaves and stems is more marked when they are bruised.

Foeniculum vulgare young foliage.

Fennel is not difficult to grow on most soils, though a deep, moist but well-drained one is the best, allied to a sunny place. Only in really severe winters will it be killed. Division every four years is usually recommended but the roots are so large and go down so deep that, if it appears healthy, it is better to let well alone. Seed will self-sow.

Freesia

The winter-flowering forms of freesia have to be grown with protection, but there are now summer-flowering versions which can be planted in mid spring outdoors, for flowering late summer. The corms are 'prepared' in the same way as hyacinths are for Christmas flowering. They are just as fragrant and with similar colours of golden, white, pink, blue and purple on stems up to 45cm (1½ft) long.

Give them well-drained soil, a sunny position, and plant about 5cm (2in) deep and 10cm (4in) apart. Increase is not possible, and the corms should be discarded once flowering is over.

Genista

This genus of plants is also known as broom, like the cytisus, and is closely related to it, being of the same pea family (*Leguminosae*). Two that are often grown are *G. hispanica*, commonly and confusingly known as the Spanish gorse, and *G. aetnensis*, the Mount Etna broom. *G. hispanica* has golden flowers in short-stalked clusters from late spring through early summer, their pineapple perfume

being most noticeable on hot sunny days. It is spiny, and grows to about 60cm (2ft) tall, unlike the Mount Etna broom, which towers to 3.5m (12ft) under favourable conditions, in a sheltered garden. Its yellow flowers in midsummer are reminiscent of vanilla in their fragrance.

If you have poor, sandy soil, it will suit these two brooms very well, especially if the site is protected and sunny. Prune after flowering to remove the flowered growth, but not too hard. Increase from seed.

Genista aetnensis.

Hamamelis mollis

The witch-hazel flowers in early and mid winter, and is strongly fragrant, scenting the air around it. The untidy, stemless flowers are formed from spidery yellow petals along the length of the young shoots. 'Pallida' has pale yellow flowers, 'Jelena' is deep red in the centre, to yellow at the end of the petals, the general affect being orange. Witch-hazel is slow-growing, to about 3m (10ft) in height and width in fifteen years; it needs good drainage, sun or a little shade, and prefers a neutral to acid soil. Pruning is not necessary. Increase by layering.

Freesias – highly scented.

Hamamelis mollis, **witch-hazel.**

Helichrysum angustifolium

Commonly called the curry plant, its leaves have a strong aroma of curry, given off profusely on hot sunny days. Unfortunately, this is not apparent if the leaves are used in food. It is a silvery-grey plant with narrow leaves, to about 60 × 60cm (2 × 2ft) when fully grown, and is one of the hardiest of its type, provided it has well-drained soil and sun. Dull yellow flowers appear in midsummer, but the stems are better pruned off before they run up to flower, to maintain the silvery appearance of the plant. Plant in spring and increase from heeled, semi-ripe cuttings taken in mid- to late summer.

Heliotropium peruvianum

Cherry pie or heliotrope is a heavily scented half-hardy annual, once much used for bedding schemes by the Victorians. Not often seen now, which is a pity when it is so fragrant; the one listed in seed cata-

Heliotrope 'Lord Roberts'.

logues is 'Marine', deep purple. Others are in cultivation such as 'Lord Roberts', dark blue, and 'White Lady', but tend to circulate via garden society seed-exchanges and private gardens. Sow in gentle heat in early spring, and plant out in the early summer in a sunny place 30cm (1ft) apart. It will flower all summer on stems 45cm (1½ft) tall.

Hemerocallis flava, daylily.

Hosta plantaginea **has scented flowers in late summer.**

Hemerocallis flava

The daylilies are usually grown as hybrids in a variety of colours, including yellow, orange, brick-red, pink and crimson. But none is scented, as this species is. *H. flava* is lemon-yellow, with much more slender growth, narrow leaves to 60cm (2ft), and stems about 75–90cm (2½-3ft) tall; flowering is from late spring to midsummer. Easily grown but preferring moist soil; sun or a little shade will suit it. Increase by division.

Hesperis matronalis

Once commonly called dame's rocket or dame's violet, and now more often known as sweet rocket, hesperis is a member of the same plant family as the wallflower and the stock and has a similar fragrance, sweet and strong, especially in the evening. The white or lilac flowers are small, in clusters appearing in early summer on stems about 60cm (2ft) tall.

It does well in dry places, and will seed into crevices in walls and between paving stones. A perennial, it is grown from seed, if single, sown in spring and transplanted in midsummer; there used to be a double form which is increased by tip cuttings or by division.

Hosta plantaginea

The plantain lilies are unscented except for this species, which has fragrant, white, funnel-shaped flowers in late summer to early autumn. The form 'Royal Standard' goes on flowering until October, on 45cm (1½ft) tall stems. The great merit of this plant is that it will grow and flower in quite deep shade but, like all hostas, it is very attractive to slugs and snails in spring as the leaves are coming through. The handsome leaves are up to 50cm (20in) long and 15cm (6in) wide. Moist, fertile soil is required; increase by division in spring.

Hyacinthus orientalis

One of the most fragrant of the flowering bulbs, hyacinth perfume will be wafted all round the garden on a warm spring day. All colours are present, depending on the variety, generally in pastel shades of blue, pink, yellow, apricot and salmon.

Some good named varieties include 'Pink Pearl', 'Delft Blue', Salmonetta', 'L'Innocence', white, 'City of Haarlem', pale yellow, 'Mulberry Rose', wine and pink. Even more fragrant, and earlier flowering, are the varieties of *H. o. albulus* or Roman hyacinths. Plant bulbs 15cm (6in) deep and 20cm (8in) apart in early to mid autumn, in humusy soil and sun or a little shade. Easily increased from offsets.

Iris

The bearded irises are a mixture of hybrids among whose parentage is *I. pallida,* and it is this that is responsible for their strong perfume, which can be of lily of the valley, vanilla, gardenia, orange blossom or chocolate! Their exquisitely beautiful flowers are unrivalled, and their only drawback is their fleeting season of 3–4 weeks in late spring and early summer.

The choice of varieties is so great it is best to visit an iris supplier or an iris show when the plants are in flower. Plant after flowering, between midsummer and the early autumn, in sun and with good drainage; only half-cover the rhizomes and divide them at the same season for increase.

Bearded iris 'Jane Phillips' which flowers in early summer.

Jasminum

The white jasmines are renowned for their fragrance on tropical nights in eastern countries, but they can be just as fragrant here, provided a sheltered, sunny planting site is supplied. *J. officinale* is one that will grow outdoors on a south-facing wall or fence; *J. polyanthum* is winter-flowering, with a few more in early summer, but needs protection. *J.* × *stephanense* has pale pink flowers. All are vigorous climbers with pinnate leaves.

Prune mainly to thin and keep within bounds at any time. Plant in spring – most soils are suitable – and increase by layering or by semi-ripe cuttings in summer.

Jasminum officinale needs sun.

Winter-flowering J. polyanthum.

Laburnum x watereri 'Vossii'.

Laburnum

The best species to buy is *L.* 'Vossii'; its yellow flowers are produced in long, drooping clusters, 25–50cm (10–20in) long in early summer, and it produces few seeds, fortunate since they are poisonous – more so than the rest of the tree. Height is about 4.5m (15ft).

Laburnums are easily accommodated trees, doing well in most soils, in sun or some shade. Not long-lived, however, they need staking in their early life, especially in windy areas. Plant in late autumn to early spring. Increase by layering. Their pliable stems make it easy for them to be trained over arches and if space allows, a succession of these makes a spectacular tunnel when the trees are in full flower.

Lathyrus odoratus

It would be difficult to find a more sweetly fragrant flower than the sweet pea, when you can find a fragrant hybrid, but many of the modern ones have been bred for colour and size only; such a pity when so much of the attraction of a sweet pea is its perfume. Wafted on the air on a sunny day, it seems to carry the essence of summer in its fragrance.

Some scented hybrids are: 'Captain Scott', white; 'Cream Southbourne'; 'Mrs C. Kay', lavender; 'Noel Sutton', blue; 'Percy Thrower', lilac and white; 'Pluto', deep blue; 'Xenia Field', pink and cream. Sow seed in pots in mid autumn and overwinter in a frame, then plant out in March, in deep fertile soil and a sunny place, 30cm (1ft) apart. Allow two sideshoots to grow, each trained up 2.1m (7ft) canes. Attach with the aid of split rings, removing the tendrils and sideshoots.

The much-loved fragrant lavender.

Lavandula

An old and much-loved fragrant shrub, lavender has been grown and used for centuries, since at least the time of the Romans. It is a Mediterranean plant but nevertheless survives most winters in Britain, even severe ones, provided it is well-established and grown 'hard', that is without too fertile a soil. Height and spread are about 90cm (3ft). The grey-green leaves are evergrey, and the blue-violet flower spikes appear in midsummer, though flowering can be later. Many of the parent plants used for propagation are hybrids and include L. latifolia or spike lavender, late summer-flowering, as one of their parents. Plant in spring in a sunny, sheltered place with good drainage. Prune by clipping with shears in spring as the new growth starts. To increase, take heeled, semi-hardwood cuttings in summer.

Sweet peas – not all are scented.

Ligusticum officinalis

This is an old culinary herb much grown by monks in medieval days; it has the common name of lovage. The celery-like, dark green leaves have a strong aroma of celery and yeast combined, and its place in the garden can always be tracked down by this pungent fragrance. It is a big plant, to 2.4m (8ft) in some cases, and about 1m (3½ft) in spread, once established. It makes a handsome border plant, with flat heads of yellow-green flowers, best removed to encourage foliage growth.

Grow from seed sown in a nursery bed in autumn and transplanted the following autumn, or from pieces of root with buds on, taken in spring. The soil should be deep and moist, and in sun or shade.

Lilium

Lilies are among the most beautiful as well as the most fragrant of flowering plants. White, orange, purple, pink and yellow are the main colours, with shades and combinations of all these, especially among the Aurelian hybrids.

Not all are scented, but two that are heavily fragrant and easily grown, are L. candidum, the Madonna lily and L. regale, the regal lily. Both are white. The Madonna lily has wide-spreading trumpet flowers

in early-midsummer in clusters at the top of 1.2–1.5m (4–5ft) stems. Plant it in late summer in alkaline, moist but well-drained soil about 7.5cm (3in) deep. L. regale has long, white trumpet flowers with a yellow throat and deep pink flushing on the outside of the petals in midsummer. Height can be 1.8m (6ft), and it should be planted at least 15cm (6in) deep in a sunny place and most soils, including slightly alkaline ones, in mid autumn.

Lonicera

Honeysuckle is one of the most well-known and loved of the native flowering plants. Its fragrance perfuming the air on a moonlit night in summer is as evocative of the British scene as a rainy day – it might be said to be the equivalent of jasmine in the tropics.

The most strongly scented is still the native species L. periclymenum, which grows in the hedgerows. The cultivar 'Belgica' flowers in the late-spring to early summer, 'Serotina' midsummer into autumn. Both climb vigorously by twining up the nearest support, and do best where they get some shade during the day. Hot, dry positions are not suitable. Plant autumn to spring for preference, and increase from hardwood cuttings or by layering.

Lilium regale, regal lily.

Lonicera periclymenum 'Belgica'.

The highly scented flowers of Magnolia × soulangiana.

Magnolia

The magnolias are magnificent flowering shrubs or trees, some spring-blooming, some flowering all through summer. *M. × soulangiana* has white, goblet-shaped flowers, tinted purple at the base; they appear in mid spring, before the leaves, continuing to open until early summer – they are almost too fragrant. The height of this shrub can be 3m (10ft) and it is nearly as wide. *M. grandiflora* is a tree to 6–9m (20–30ft) and more. Its creamy white, thick-petalled flowers, 30cm (1ft) wide, appear midsummer to early autumn and scent the air for many yards around. It also makes a good evergreen shrub for walls.

Plant in humusy, well-drained soil which is neutral or acid in reaction (be careful not to damage or bruise the fleshy roots) in sun or a little shade. Can be increased by layering in summer.

37

Winter-blooming *Mahonia japonica*.

Matthiola bicornis, an annual.

Mahonia

The best of the scented mahonias is *M. japonica*, a winter-flowering evergreen shrub. The pinnate leaves have holly-like leaflets, and the lemon-yellow flowers, which are like lily of the valley flowers in shape, have a similarly strong fragrance, in early-midwinter, sometimes earlier. In spike-like clusters at the end of the shoots, they are followed by blue berries. A large shrub; height and spread can be 1.8 × 1.8m (6 × 6ft) and more. Shelter from north wind; any soil but a very heavy one, and shade, are preferable. Prune only to shape, in mid spring, and increase by cuttings – either semi-hardwood or heeled – in summer.

Matthiola

The stocks, grown in cottage gardens for hundreds of years, are hardy or half-hardy annuals, or biennials. Perhaps the most scented is the night-scented *M. bicornis*, a hardy annual, sown outdoors in its flowering site in spring. Height is about 30cm (1ft). The insignificant flowers give out a wonderful fragrance at night out of all proportion to their appearance.

Other fragrant stocks which have the added merit of attractive flowers are: the Brompton stocks, to 45cm (1½ft), with biennial spikes of double flowers in spring; ten-week stocks, summer-flowering, half-hardy annuals of densely flowered spikes, 30–75cm (1–2½ft) tall depending on strain; East Lothian stocks – also half-hardy annuals – flowering late summer to late autumn, with flowers in short spikes on plants 30cm (1ft) tall. Flower colours of all are in the range of pinks, purples and mauves, also white. Sow in spring, depending on type, and plant out accordingly, spaced at 23–30cm (9–12in), in sun or a little shade and neutral to just alkaline soil.

Melissa officinalis

The common name, lemon balm, gives this plant away. Its leaves are strongly redolent of lemon and a popular addition to summer drinks and tea, especially China tea. They are said to have a soothing and relaxing affect. Lemon balm is an easily grown herbaceous perennial which dies down in autumn; height can be 75–90cm (2½–3ft) and nearly as much wide. The creamy white flower spikes should be removed if leaves are required.

Melissa o. 'Variegata' has leaves heavily splashed with gold, much more ornamental and just as lemon-scented, but cutting the flower stems down is essential to retain good foliage. Any soil suits it; 'Variegata' needs some sun. Increase by seed or, for quickness, by simple division.

Mentha

The mints show an amazing diversity of aroma among their varieties. Garden mint, *M. × spicata* is the conventional one. Others are peppermint, *M. × piperita*, the black form of which is the most pungent – it has deep purple-black leaves and stems; Eau de Cologne Mint, *M. × piperata citrata*, distinctly perfumed and purple-flushed on the leaves. There is also pineapple mint, *M. suaveolens* 'Variegata' with irregularly white-variegated leaves; ginger mint, *M. × gentilis* 'Variegata', has yellow-striped leaves. The apple mint, *M. suaveolens*, has rounded woolly leaves; pennyroyal, *M. pulegium*, has tiny leaves, mat-like growth and a much stronger aroma than the others. All are easily grown in any soil – in fact, they need restricting or they will take over – and are increased by rooted runners from spring to autumn.

Melissa officinalis 'Variegata'.

Mentha suaveolens 'Variegata'.

Myrtus communis

Myrtle is a shrub grown since the days of classical Greece and Rome, when it was much revered and a symbol of youth and beauty. It grows to 3m (10ft), but there is a dwarf form *tarentina*, 90cm (3ft).

Myrtle is slightly tender and needs a sheltered garden; given this, it will be clothed in small, white, fragrant flowers from mid to late summer. The leaves are aromatic. Plant in sun, and average soil, and prune only if shaping is required, in late spring. Increase from seed or by semi-ripe cuttings with bottom heat.

Monarda didyma

This is a North American native, grown by the Oswego Indians; hence its alternative common name of Oswego tea. But it is better known as bergamot, from the orange aroma of the leaves. It is a herbaceous

perennial growing to 60–90cm (2–3ft) and needing 50cm (20in) of space; the red flowers appear all summer. Good varieties are 'Croftway Pink', 'Prairie Night', purple; 'Mahogany', brown-red; and 'Snow Maiden', white. Give it moist soil and sun or a little shade; increase by division in spring or autumn.

Narcissus

The most fragrant of the narcissi are the jonquils. *N. jonquilla*, from northern Portugal and the Pyrenees; *N. odorus*, the Campernelle jonquil, and the Tazetta and Poeticus groups. The jonquils grow to about 30cm (1ft) and have clusters of small shallow-cupped flowers. *N. odorus* is similar, but with a large cup and wider leaves. Tazetta narcissi are cluster-flowered, coloured orange, yellow and white, with a short cup and petals 4cm (1½in) wide, on stems up to 60cm (2ft) tall, flowering outdoors in winter in sheltered gardens, otherwise under cover.

The Poeticus narcissi flower in late spring, also having a shallow cup, orange or yellow, with petals always white, to a height of 45cm (1½ft). Plant in the late summer to early autumn, 10–12.5cm (4–5in) deep, in most soils and sun or shade. Increase by offsets.

Myrtus communis, **or myrtle.**

A jonquil narcissus.

Nepeta cataria

This is the true catmint, or catnep, with strongly aromatic leaves reminiscent of mint. Its attraction for cats is legendary but it is said that when it is grown from seed they ignore it; grown from transplants or rooted cuttings, they will roll on it and generally destroy it. In fact, any bruising or injury releases the aroma, more likely with transplanting than with seeds.

The toothed leaves are downy, and the white or light pink flowers, on stems about 60cm (2ft) tall, last from midsummer to autumn. Any soil and some sun suit it; increase by division in spring/autumn.

Nicotiana alata

The tobacco plant is a half-hardy annual that grows into quite a large plant for an annual, about 75cm (2½ft) tall and 45cm (1½ft) wide, with leaves up to 12.5cm (5in) long on branching side stems. But the newer mixtures are shorter, 23–45cm (9–18in), and do not need staking. The tubular flowers open out into petal-like segments and are fragrant, especially at night and particularly this white species and white varieties from it.

Other colours are red, wine, yellow, purple, pink and magenta; 'Lime Green' is exactly that colour but unscented. *N. tabacum* is the plant whose leaves are used for cigarettes. Sow in gentle heat in early to mid spring, and plant out after hardening off in early summer. Average soil and sun or light shade are suitable; spacing is approximately 23–45cm (9–18in).

Nicotiana alata comes in various colours.

Oenothera

The evening primroses derive their common name from the yellow of their saucer-shaped flowers and the fact that they perfume the air in the evening when they open. *O. biennis* is a native biennial, flowering from early summer into early autumn, height 1.2–1.8m (4–6ft). *O. missouriensis* is perennial, 15–23cm (6–9in) tall, with very large flowers in late summer. The perennial 'Fireworks' has red buds, and purple-tinged leaves, to 45cm (1½ft) tall. Any soil – preferably well-drained – and plenty of sun suit it; increase by division in spring, but you can also grow *O. missouriensis* and *O. biennis* from seed.

Osmanthus delavayi

An evergreen shrub, growing slowly to about 90cm (3ft) tall in ten years; rounded in shape and with dark green leaves forming a dense cover. The small, tubular, white flowers are intensely fragrant and open in mid spring. *O. heterophyllus* has holly-like leaves and grows to about 1.5m (5ft), flowering in early autumn. To be at their best, they need shelter from north and east; otherwise, most soils and sun or a little shade suit them. No pruning is necessary; increase by cuttings in summer or layering in autumn.

Oenothera missouriensis.

Paeonia lactiflora

This and its garden varieties are the scented forms of peony. It comes from northern China, Mongolia and Siberia, and is extremely hardy. The hybrids are among the most beautiful of herbaceous perennials. A few good varieties are: 'Sarah Bernhardt' pink; 'Felix Crousse' deep red; 'Festiva Maxima' white, all double; 'Bowl of Beauty' an exquisite single with pink outer petals and a mass of creamy yellow central stamens. Many more are listed in catalogues and flowering is in early-midsummer. Height is 75–90cm (2½-3ft).

Plant in early autumn, or mid spring; put the crown about 2.5cm (1in) below the surface, and grow in deep moist soil and sun, or a little shade, spaced 60cm (2ft) apart. Mulch every spring. Increase by careful division in spring.

Paeonia 'Bowl of Beauty'.

Philadelphus coronarius 'Aureus'.

Pelargonium

There is a group of pelargoniums which has scented or aromatic leaves, varying remarkably in their fragrance. Their flowers are small, nothing like as spectacular as the regal and zonal hybrids, but still ornamental, mostly white, lilac or rose-pink. They include: *P. crispum* 'Variegatum', lilac with strongly lemon-scented, grey-green leaves edged cream; 'Paton's Unique', rose-scented and pink; 'Attar of Roses', also rose-scented, pink; 'Clorinda', eucalyptus aroma, red and purple; 'Prince of Orange', orange-scented, lilac. Plant outdoors only in summer, in full sun and with good drainage; increase from cuttings.

Philadelphus

Not all the mock orange blossoms (syringa) are scented, as is generally thought, but *P. coronarius*, the commonly grown one is, and very strongly, too. Height can be 3m (10ft) and spread easily 1.8m (6ft). Its creamy white, golden-centred flowers appear in early summer. 'Belle Etoile' is smaller, 1.8m (6ft),

spread 1.5m (5ft), and has strongly perfumed white flowers blotched purple at the base. 'Manteau d'Hermine' is 90cm (3ft), double creamy white. Grow in any average soil and sun or light shade; increase by hardwood cuttings. Prune directly after flowering to remove some of the flowered shoots.

Phlox

The phlox are good late summer-flowering herbaceous perennials, with a fragrance unlike any other plant, but not universally popular. However, to many people it is evocative of long, hot summer days and a favourite on that account, added to which it is extremely decorative.

There are many beautiful hybrids: 'Starfire', deep red; 'The King', violet-purple; 'Balmoral', pink; 'White Admiral'; and 'Sandringham', cyclamen pink, are a few. Average height is 90cm (3ft) and spread is 75cm (2½ft). Phlox like a moist soil and will grow in shade as well as sun. Increase by division in spring or autumn, or by root cuttings in winter.

The border phlox 'Sandringham'.

43

Primula

This is an enormous genus of at least 500 species, plus all their attendant varieties. Many are fragrant: *P. vulgaris*, the primrose, 15cm (6in), has an evanescent woodland fragrance in mid spring; *P. auricula*, 15–23cm (6–9in), both Show and Border hybrids are heavily fragrant mid to late spring, the latter being perfectly hardy and suited to outdoor cultivation. *P. florindae*, 60cm (2ft), shows off its yellow, bell-shaped, scented flowers to best advantage in summer in the bog-garden. *P. chionantha*, 30–38cm (12–15in), is creamy white, the leaves dusted with white. *P. sikkimensis*, 30cm (1ft), is pale yellow, its bell-shaped flowers hanging in clusters in summer, and *P. veris*, 23cm (9in), the native British cowslip, is delightfully fragrant, and coloured yellow or sometimes brickred, in mid spring.

All prefer moist, humusy soil and a little shade; plant in early autumn and increase from seed, or by division after flowering if spring flowering, or in early autumn.

Reseda odorata

Mignonette means 'little darling' in French, and it was the French who grew it in pots on the balconies and terraces of their homes during the last century, following the example of the Empress Josephine in the previous century. The greenish-brown flowers are inconspicuous, in fat spikes about 15cm (6in) long, but their strong fragrance pervades the air, especially on sunny days and it is a popular plant with bees. Height is about 30cm (1ft). Sow seed outdoors each year in spring and thin to 23cm (9in); it likes sun and an alkaline soil.

Rhododendron

Most are not scented at all, but two

Reseda odorata, mignonette.

that are fragrant are *R. luteum* and *R.* 'Fragrantissimum'. The former is a yellow azalea, sometimes called the honeysuckle azalea, with long, prominent stamens protruding from the funnel-shaped flowers; the latter is white, tinted rose-pink. Both flower in late spring; *R.* 'Fragrantissimum' is the earlier of the two, sometimes flowering in mid spring in sheltered gardens. Grow in acid soil and dappled shade such as that cast by light woodland. Expect them to grow to about 2.1 × 1.8m (7 × 6ft); increase by layering in summer.

Rosa

There are many, many species, varieties and hybrids of roses that are fragrant, and one can only mention a few of the most scented and best known here. All the hybrid musks are delightful, such as 'Felicia', pink and salmon, and 'Penelope', creamy pink. The Damask roses such as the striped, pale pink and white 'York and Lancaster'; the Cabbage roses (centifolia) e.g. 'Fantin Latour', pale pink to blush; the

44

Hybrid musk rose 'Penelope'.

Bourbons, 'Mme Isaac Pereire', deep pink is an example; $R. \times alba$ and its hybrids; *R. gallica* and hybrids such as 'Tuscany Superb', which is a deep velvety purple.

Among the modern roses are: 'Fragrant Cloud', coral red; 'Wendy Cussons', rose and silver; 'Blue Moon', purple and 'Tynwald', white; all large-flowered (hybrid tea). 'Dearest', salmon; 'Chinatown', deep yellow, 'Troika', bronze-yellow, and 'Iceberg', white, are cluster-flowered (floribunda).

Roses grow in most soils with reasonable drainage and with sun for most of the day – a little shade is advisable at some time. Prune the large-flowered kinds in early spring to reduce shoots by half their length. Also prune cluster-flowered kinds but cut the oldest shoots back to ground level. Old shrub roses need not be pruned except to remove dead and crowded growth. They can be increased by hardwood cuttings, seed, layering in summer and budding in midsummer.

Rosa x alba, **white rose of York.**

Hybrid tea rose 'Fragrant Cloud'.

Skimmia

The cultivar *S. japonica* 'Fragrans' is the one with scented flowers, small and white, appearing in early mid spring. It is evergreen and quite small, to about 90cm (3ft) and not quite as much wide, and prefers a little shade. Any reasonable soil will suit, and pruning is not required except to remove winter-damaged shoots in early spring. Increase by semi-ripe cuttings in summer.

Thymus

The thymes are heavily aromatic when the sun is shining full on them, and they are growing in poor stony soil. Natives of the Mediterranean region, they are surprisingly hardy in Britain, and have the merit of being evergreen. *T. vulgaris* is the common species, about 15cm (6in) tall, with tiny pink-purple flowers in late spring-early summer; *T.* × *citriodorus* has lemon-scented larger leaves on plants about 23cm (9in) tall, and *T. herba-barona* is redolent of caraway, as well as thyme, given off when trodden on; it forms mats of tiny leaves on creeping stems. Increase from cuttings, and rooted stems or layers.

Ulex europaeus

Gorse flowers practically all year round, its golden-yellow flowers clothing very spiny bushes up to 1.8m (6ft) tall and 1.2m (4ft) wide. Hot sun brings out its vanilla-like fruity perfume to the full, and indeed it should always be grown in a really sunny position. A south-facing bank is ideal, where the drainage is good, especially if the soil is poor and stony. 'Plenus' is a smaller, double-flowered form. Increase from semi-ripe cuttings in summer, and clip to neaten in late spring if required.

Verbena

Among the most fragrant of flowers, verbena hybrids are half-hardy annuals with small, primrose-like flowers in clusters at the end of 15–30cm (6–12in) stems from early to late summer. Colours range through pinks, reds, purples, white and blue, some with a white 'eye'. The white ones have the strongest scent, and Showtime is a strain all of whose flowers have some perfume. Sow in a little heat in early spring, and plant out in late spring, in a sunny site and any reasonable soil.

Bedding verbena 'Derby'.

Ulex europaeus **or gorse.**

46

Viburnum

This is a large and varied genus of shrubs, some of whose species are scented. *V. fragrans* flowers in winter and has tiny white flowers in clusters on leafless shoots. *V.* × *bodnantense* is taller, with larger, pink flowers, red in bud, but is a rather angular and gaunt-looking shrub. The smaller *V. fragrans,* to about 2.1m (7ft) is a much more pleasing shape. If space is restricted, *V. carlesii* is preferable, as height is only about 1.2–1.8m (4–6ft); its strongly scented white flowers come in clusters 7.5cm (3in) wide at the end of the shoots in mid to late spring.

Most soils are suitable, with plenty of humus; sun is necessary. No pruning is required; increase by semi-ripe cuttings in summer or alternatively by layering in autumn.

Viola odorata, **sweet violet.**

Viola odorata

The sweet violet is a native plant having one of the most intense and individual perfumes of any flower. The white form, *alba,* is even stronger, and there is an autumn-flowering kind called *V. o. praecox,* which will flower intermittently through winter as well.

Light shade and a fertile, well-drained soil suit them best; keep well-watered in dry weather. Increase by dividing clumps in spring or autumn, or by detaching runners.

Wisteria

The most widely grown species is *W. sinensis,* a vigorous climber to 30m (100ft), and smelling strongly of vanilla, especially on sunny days. *W. floribunda* 'Macrobotrys' is less rampant, and has flower clusters of violet blue up to 60cm (2ft) long, but is less fragrant than the Chinese version.

A deep, moist soil is important, together with a sunny wall, and shelter from cold and wind; supply strong supports. Plant from containers and do not be surprised if it takes several years before it starts to climb. Some do so at once, others may take seven years. Prune sideshoots in late midsummer to 15cm (6in) and again in early winter to one or two buds. Cut leaders back to fit the space available.

Viburnum carlesii.

INDEX AND ACKNOWLEDGEMENTS

Picture credits

Pat Brindley: 8, 11(bl), 12(r), 24(t, b), 28(r), 29(t), 30(r), 31(b), 34(tr), 38(tr), 42(bl, br), 42(l, r), 45(b), 47(l).
John Glover: 1, 6 (t, b), 11(br).
Iris Hardwick: 10, 45(t).
S & O Mathews: 7(t), 9(bl).
Harry Smith Horticultural Photographic Collection: 4/5, 7(b), 9(br), 12(l), 13, 22/3, 25(t, b), 26(t, b), 27(l, r), 28(l), 29(b), 30(l), 31(t), 32(tl, tr), 33, 34(tl, b), 35(tr, bl), 36(bl, br), 37, 38(tl), 39(bl, br), 40(bl, br), 41, 43(l, r), 44, 46(l, r), 47(r).
Michael Warren: 45(c).

Artwork by Simon Roulstone